Cardis to
CROCHET

Complete Instructions for **5 Projects**

Creative Publishing
international

Contents

ribbon-yarn **jacket**

What is your favorite color? Can't decide? Crochet a versatile jacket using yarn that continually changes color to display an entire rainbow of jewel tones throughout the fabric. This jacket, made from cotton/rayon ribbon yarn, has an open shell-stitch pattern that will dress you up but not heat you up.

yarn
Medium-weight ribbon

1x & 2x: 1,200 yd (1,098 m)
3x & 4x: 1,600 yd (1,464 m)

hooks
8/H (5 mm) for main body
6/G (4 mm) for trim

stitches
Single crochet
Double crochet

gauge
2 shell groups = 4"
(10.2 cm) using 8/H hook

notions
Tapestry needle
Five buttons, ¾" (1.9 cm)
diameter
Hand-sewing needle
Thread

finished size
1X (2X, 3X, 4X)
Bust size 46" (50", 54½", 58½")
[116.8 (127, 138.4, 148.6) cm]

notes

Single Crochet Decreases (sc2tog)

To dec, *pick up lp in next st, yo, pick up lp in next st, yo and pull through all 3 lps on hook.*

back

Foundation row: With 8/H hook, ch 63 (69, 75, 81). Starting in second ch from hook, 1 sc in each ch across, turn—62 (68, 74, 80) sts.

Row 1 (RS): Ch 5 (counts as dc, ch 1), sk 1 st, 1 dc in next st (half CL made), * ch 2, sk 2 sts, 1 sc next st, ch 2, sk 2 sts, [1 dc, ch 1, 1 dc, ch 1, 1 dc] in next st (full CL made), rep from * 8 (9, 10, 11) times more, ending with ch 2, sk 2 sts, 1 sc next st, ch 2, sk 2 sts, [1 dc, ch 1, 1 dc] in tch (half CL made), turn. There will be 9 (10, 11, 12) full CL and one half CL each side.

Row 2: Ch 1, 1 sc in same st, * ch 2, 1 CL in next sc, ch 2, 1 sc in second dc of next CL, rep from * 9 (10, 11, 12) more, ending ch 2, 1 sc in third ch of tch, turn—10 (11, 12, 13) full CL.

Row 3: Ch 5 (counts as dc, ch 1), 1 dc same st (half CL) * ch 2, 1 sc in center dc of next CL, ch 2, 1 CL in next sc, rep from * 8 (9, 10, 11) times more, ending ch 2, 1 sc in center of next CL, ch 2, [1 dc, ch 1, 1 dc] in top of tch (half CL), turn. There will be 9 (10, 11, 12) full CL and one half CL each side.

Rep rows 2 and 3 until piece measures 13½" (14", 14½", 15") [34.3 (35.6, 36.8, 38.1) cm] from beg, ending with row 2.

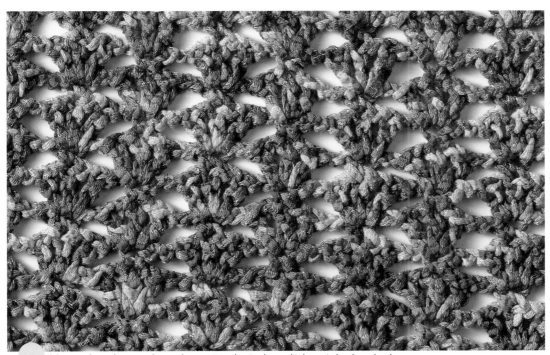

Double crochet clusters throughout give the jacket a lightweight, lacy look.

Armhole shaping: Sl st over first half CL, ch-sp, sc, ch-sp, full CL, ch-sp, and sc, ch 4 (counts as dc, ch 1), [1 dc, ch 1, 1 dc] in same st (new CL formed), * ch 2, sc in center of next CL, ch 2, 1 CL in next sc, rep from * 6 (7, 8, 9) times more, turn, leave rem st unworked—8 (9, 10, 11) CL.

Next row: Ch 1, sc2tog, * ch 2, CL in next sc, ch 2, sc in center of next CL, rep from * 5 (6, 7, 8) times more, 1 CL in next sc, ch 2, sc2tog, 1 sc in top of tch, turn.

Cont pattern as established on rem sts until armhole measures 9½" (10", 10½", 11") [24.1 (25.4, 26.9, 27.9) cm]. Fasten off.

left front

Foundation row: With 8/H hook, ch 33 (39, 45, 51). Work as back on 32 (38, 44, 50) sts. There will be 4 (5, 6, 7) full CL and one half CL each side on patt row 3. Work even in patt as established until same length as back to armhole, ending with row 2.

Armhole shaping: Sl st over first half CL, ch-sp, sc, ch-sp, full CL, ch-sp, and sc, ch 4 (counts as dc, ch 1, [1 dc, ch 1, 1 dc] in same st (new CL formed), * ch 2, sc in center of next CL, ch 2, 1 CL in next sc, rep from * 1 (2, 3, 4) times more, ending ch 2, 1 sc in center of next CL, ch 2, [1 dc, ch 1, 1 dc] in top of tch (half CL), turn—3 (4, 5, 6) CL and one half CL at front edge.

Next row: Ch 1, 1 sc in same st, * ch 2, CL in next sc, ch 2, sc in center of next CL, rep from * 1 (2, 3, 4) times more, 1 CL in next sc, ch 2, sc2tog, 1 sc in top of tch, turn.

Cont to work even on rem sts until armhole measures 7" (7½", 8", 8½"), [17.8 (19.1, 20.3, 21.6) cm] ending with row 2.

Neck shaping: Work patt across row, leaving last (sc, ch-sp, CL, ch-sp, sc, ch-sp, CL, ch-sp) unworked for neck, turn. Cont patt as established on rem sts until armhole measures 9½" (10", 10½", 11") [24.1 (25.4, 26.9, 27.9) cm]. Fasten off.

right front

Work as for left front, reversing armhole and neck shaping.

sleeves

Make 2.

Foundation row: With 6/G hook, ch 33 (39, 44, 50). Work in sc on 32 (38, 43, 49) sts for 5 rows. Change to patt as for back for 2 rows. Change to 8/H hook and cont patt until piece measures 8" (20.3 cm) from beg, ending with row 2, turn.

First increase row (on patt row 3): Ch 5 (counts as dc, ch 1), work [1 dc, ch 1, 1 dc] in same sp forming new CL, work patt as established to end of row, work [1 dc, ch 1, 1 dc, ch 1, 1 dc] in top of tch (full CL made), turn—5 (6, 7, 8) full CL on patt row 3 instead of 4 (5, 6, 7) CL and one half CL each side.

Second increase row: Ch 5 (counts as dc, ch 1), 1 dc in same st (half CL), ch 2, 1 sc in next dc, ch 2, 1 CL in next sc, cont patt as established to last sc, CL in last sc, ch 2, sc in next dc, ch 2, [1 dc, ch 2, 1 dc] in tch (half CL), turn—5 (6, 7, 8) full CL and one half CL each side.

Keeping inc sts in patt, work 4 rows even.

Rep last 6 rows, until you have 7 (8, 9, 10) full CL, half CL each side. Work even until 16" (16½", 17", 17½") [40.6 (41.9, 43.2, 44.5) cm] from beg, ending with row 2.

Sleeve cap: Sl st over first half CL, ch-sp, sc, ch-sp, full CL, ch-sp, and sc, ch 4 (counts as dc, ch 1), [1 dc, ch 1, 1 dc] in same st (new CL formed), * ch 2, sc in center of next CL, ch 2, 1 CL in next sc, rep from * 4 (5, 6, 7) times more, turn, leave rem sts unworked—6 (7, 8, 9) CL.

Next row: Ch 1, sc2tog, * ch 2, CL in next sc, ch 2, sc in center of next CL, rep from * 4 (5, 6, 7) times more, 1 CL in next sc, ch 2, sc2tog, 1 sc in top of tch, turn.

Cont to work even until sleeve cap is 4" (4½", 5", 5½") [10.2 (11.4, 12.7, 14) cm]. Change to 6/G hook, work 2" (5.1 cm) more. Fasten off.

finishing

1. Sew shoulder seams.
2. Mark center of sleeve cap, pin center of sleeve to shoulder seam, pin underarms in place, sew in sleeve, easing in to fit.
3. Sew underarm seams.
4. Work front and neck border.
5. Sew on buttons opposite buttonholes.
6. Weave in ends using a tapestry needle.
7. Do not block.

front and neck border

Row 1: Using 6/G hook, starting at bottom right front, RS facing you, sc evenly spaced along right front, 3 sc in last st on front to form corner, cont around neck, 3 sc in top of left front to form corner, cont down left front to bottom, turn.

Row 2: Ch 1, sk first st, 1 sc in each sc just worked, working 3 sc in center st of each corner, turn.

Row 3 (buttonhole row): Before beg row, place pins on right front, marking 5 buttonholes evenly spaced, allowing 2 sts for each buttonhole. Work in sc to first marker, * ch 2, sk 2 sts, 1 sc in each sc to next marker, rep from * 3 times more, ch 2, sk 2, cont in sc, working 3 sc in corner st, cont around neck, 3 sc in corner st, cont down left front, turn.

Row 4: Ch 1, sk first st, 1 sc in each sc worked, working 3 sc in each corner and 2 sc in each ch-2 sp to complete buttonhole, turn.

Row 5: Rep row 2, fasten off.

Several rows of single crochet stabilize the neckline, sleeve ends, and button bands.

alpaca appliqué **cardigan**

Few pleasures in life can top the soft, cozy warmth of an alpaca sweater. This classic cardigan is sure to become one of your favorites. The floral appliqués arranged asymmetrically around the neckline draw all eyes to your beaming smile.

yarn
Lightweight alpaca 🧶3
Color A:
1x & 2x: 1,500 yd (1,380 m)
3x: 1,625 yd (1,495 m)
4x: 1,750 yd (1,610 m)
Color B:
125 yd (115 m)
Color C:
125 yd (115 m)

hooks
9/I (5.5 mm) for main body
8/H (5 mm) for trim

stitches
Single crochet
Single crochet through
the back loop
Single crochet through
the front loop
Half double crochet
Double crochet
Reverse single crochet

gauge
13 dc = 4" (10.2 cm) using 9/I
hook

notions
Tapestry needle
Five buttons, ¾" (1.9 cm)
diameter
Hand-sewing needle
Thread

finished size
1X (2X, 3X, 4X)
Bust size 47" (50", 52", 55")
[119.4 (127, 132.1, 139.7) cm]

notes

1. **Single Crochet Decreases (sc2tog)**
   (a) At beg of row: Ch 1, turn, sk first st, pick up lp in next st, yo, pick up lp in next st, yo and pull through all 3 lps on hook.
   (b) At end of row: Work to last 3 sts, pick up lp in next st, yo, pick up lp in next st, yo and pull through all 3 lps on hook, 1 sc in tch.
2. **Single Crochet Increases**
   (a) At beg of row: Ch 1, sk first st, work 2 sc in next st.
   (b) At end of row: Work to last 2 sts, 2 sc in next st, 1 sc in tch.
3. **Double Crochet Decreases (dc2tog)**
   (a) To dec at beg of row, sk first st after beg chain, yoh, pick up lp in next st, yo and through 2 lps, yo, pick up lp in next st, yo, pull through 2 lps, yo and pull through all 3 lps on hook.
   (b) To dec at end of row, work until last 3 sts on row, yoh, pick up lp in next st, yo and pull through 2 lps, yo, pick up lp in next st, yo, pull through 2 lps, yo, pull through all 3 lps on hook, dc in top of tch.
4. **Double Crochet Increases**
   (a) At beg of row: Ch 3 turn, sk first st, work 2 dc in next st.
   (b) At end of row: Work to last 2 sts, 2 dc in next st, 1 dc in tch.

back

Foundation row: With A and 9/I hook, ch 76 (80, 84, 88). Starting in second ch from hook, work 1 sc in each ch across row, turn—75 (79, 83, 87) sc.

Row 1 (RS): Ch 3 (counts as dc), sk first sc, 1 dc in next 73 (77, 81, 85) sc, 1 dc in top of tch, turn—75 (79, 83, 87) dc.

Row 2: Ch 1 (counts as sc), sk first dc, 1 sc in next 73 (77, 81, 85) dc, 1 sc in top of tch, turn.

Rep rows 1 and 2 until piece measures 12" (12½", 13", 13½") [30.5 (31.8, 33, 34.3) cm] from beg, ending with row 1.

Armhole shaping: Sl st over 6 sts, work sc over next 63 (67, 71, 75), leave rem 6 sts unworked, turn.

Alternating rows of single and double crochet stitches make up the sweater body.

Cont in patt, dec 1 st each edge every row 3 times—57 (61, 65, 69) sts. Cont in patt until armhole measures 8" (8½", 9", 9½") [20.3 (21.6, 22.9, 24.1) cm], ending with row 1.

Right shoulder shaping (WS): Sc across next 19 (20, 21, 22), turn, leave rem sts unworked. Cont in patt, dec 1 st at neck edge every row 5 times—14 (15, 16, 17) sts.

Work even on rem 14 (15, 16, 17) until armhole measures 10" (10½", 11", 11½") [25.4 (26.9, 27.9, 29.2) cm]. Fasten off.

Left shoulder shaping: With WS facing, sk center 19 (21, 23, 25) sts, join yarn and work rem 19 (20, 21, 22) sts. Cont in patt, dec 1 st at neck edge every row 5 times. Work even until shoulder measures same length as right shoulder. Fasten off.

left front

Foundation row: With A and 9/I hook, ch 40 (42, 44, 46). Work as for back on 39 (41, 43, 45) sts until piece measures same length as back to armhole, ending with row 1.

Armhole shaping (WS): Work sc in next 33 (35, 37, 39) sts, turn, leave rem 6 sts unworked. Cont in patt, dec 1 st at side edge every row row 3 times—30 (32, 34, 36) sts.

Cont in patt as established on rem 30 (32, 34, 36) sts until armhole is 5½" (6", 6½", 7") [14 (15.2, 16.5, 17.8) cm], ending with row 2.

Neck shaping:
Next row (RS): Cont in patt to last 13 (14, 15, 16) sts, turn, leave rem sts unworked for neck. Cont in patt, dec 1 st at neck edge every row 3 times. Work even on rem 14 (15, 16, 17) sts until piece measures same length as back to shoulder. Fasten off.

right front

Work same as for left front to the beg of armhole shaping.

Next row (WS): Sl st across first 6 sts, work rem sts, turn.

Cont in patt, dec 1 st at side edge every row 3 times—30 (32, 34, 36) sts.

Work even until piece measures same length as left front to beg of neck shaping, ending with row 2.

Next row (RS): Sl st over 13 (14, 15, 16) sts, work in patt to end of row.

Cont in patt, dec 1 st at neck edge every row 3 times. Work even on rem 14 (15, 16, 17) sts until same length as left front. Fasten off.

Single crochet rows form the stable border around the neck and the front button bands.

sleeves

Make 2.

Foundation row: With A and 8/H hook, ch 39 (41, 43, 45). Work in patt on 38 (40, 42, 44) sts for 4 rows.

Change to 9/I hook. Cont in patt for 3 more rows. Inc 1 st each edge on next row and every sc row 11 (12, 13, 14) times more—60 (64, 68, 72) sts. Cont in patt until sleeve measures 16" (16½", 17", 17½") [40.6 (41.9, 43.2, 44.5) cm] from beg, ending with row 1.

Sleeve cap (WS): Sl st over 6 sts, cont in patt to last 6 sts, leave rem sts unworked. Cont in patt, dec 1 st at each edge every other row until 20 sts rem. Fasten off.

paisley motif

Make 3 with B.

Foundation: With 8/H hook, ch 4, Sl st to first ch to form ring. Do not turn.

Rnd 1: Ch 3 (counts as dc), work 11 dc in ring, Sl st to top of beg ch 3 to join. Do not turn. Note: From this point on, you will be working back and forth in rows, not in rnds.

Row 2: Ch 1, working in BL only, work 1 sc in next 2 dc, work 2 hdc in next 3 dc, 2 dc in each of next 3 dc—14 sts. Leave rem sts unworked. Do not turn.

Row 3: Ch 1, working in FL only (you will work in BL of these sts in row 4), work 1 rev sc in 14 sts of previous row. Do not turn.

Row 4: Working in BL only of same sts worked in row 3, work 1 sc in each of first 2 sts, 2 hdc in each of next 3 sts, 2 dc in each of next 3 sts—14 sts. Leave rem sts unworked. Do not turn.

Row 5: Rep row 3.

Repeat rows 4 and 5 once more. Fasten off, leaving 12" (30.5 cm) tail of yarn for sewing.

flower motif

Make 4 with B.

Foundation row: With 8/H hook, * ch 9. Starting in third ch from hook, work [1 sc, 1 hdc] in next ch, 1 dc in next 3 ch, 1 hdc in next ch, 1 sc in last ch, do not turn. Rep from * 7 times more —8 petals total. Sl st in last st of first petal to join into flower. Fasten off, leaving 12" (30.5 cm) tail of yarn for sewing.

Flowers, paisleys, and leaf motifs are crocheted separately and hand-stitched in an asymmetrical pattern over the shoulders and neckline.

leaf motif

Make 6 with B, 7 with C.

Foundation row: With 8/H hook, ch 16. Starting in second ch from hook, work 1 sc in next 3 ch, 1 hdc in next 3 ch, 1 dc in next 3 ch, 1 hdc in next 3 ch, 1 sc in next 3 ch. Fasten off, leaving 12" (30.5 cm) tail of yarn for sewing.

flower centers

Make 8 with C, 7 with B, 2 with A.

Foundation row: With 8/H hook, ch 4, sl st to first ch to form ring. Do not turn.

Rnd 1: Ch 1, work 12 sc in ring, Sl st to top of beg ch 1 to join. Do not turn. Fasten off, leaving 12" (30.5 cm) tail of yarn for sewing.

finishing

1. Sew shoulder seams.
2. Mark center of sleeve cap, pin center of sleeve to shoulder seam, pin underarms in place, sew in sleeve, easing in to fit.
3. Sew underarm seams.
4. Work front and neck border.
5. Sew motifs in place, using photos on pages 36–40 as a guide.
6. Sew on buttons opposite buttonholes.
7. Weave in ends using a tapestry needle.
8. Do not block.

front and neck border

Row 1: With RS facing, 8/H hook and A, join yarn at bottom right front, sc evenly spaced along right front, 3 sc in last st on front to form corner, cont around neck, 3 sc in top of left front to form corner, cont down left front to bottom, turn.

Row 2: Ch 1, sk first st, 1 sc in each sc just worked, working 3 sc in center st of each corner, turn.

Row 3 (buttonhole row): Before beg row, place pins on right front, marking 5 buttonholes evenly spaced, allowing 2 sts for each buttonhole. Work in sc to first marker, * ch 2, sk 2 sts, 1 sc in each sc to next marker, rep from * 3 times more, ch 2, sk 2, cont in sc, work 3 sc in corner st, cont around neck, 3 sc in corner st, cont down left front, turn.

Row 4: Ch 1, sk first st, 1 sc in each sc worked, working 3 sc in each corner and 2 sc in each ch-2 sp to complete buttonhole, turn.

Row 5: Rep row 2, fasten off.

silk scoop-neck **cardigan**

You'll love wearing this sweater, made with luxurious pure silk yarn in a vibrant color and wonderful stitch pattern. Petal-like clusters on a mesh background give it an ultra-feminine look.

yarn
Lightweight silk

1x & 2 x: 1,242 yd (1,134 m)
3x & 4 x: 1,380 yd (1,260 m)

hooks
5/F (3.75 mm) for main body
6/G (4 mm) for sleeve shaping
4/E (3.5 mm) for borders

stitches
Single crochet
Double crochet
Triple crochet
Triple treble crochet
Reverse single crochet

gauge
7 ch-2 spaces or 2 complete
flower clusters = 4" (10.2 cm)
using 5/F hook

notions
Tapestry needle
Three button forms, ½"
(1.3 cm) diameter

finished size
1X (2X, 3X, 4X)
Bust size 43" (49", 51", 58")
[109.2 (124.5, 129.5, 147.3) cm]

notes

1. **Triple Treble Crochet (trtr)**
   Yoh 4 times, pick up lp in next st, [yo, pull through 2 lps] 5 times.
2. **Triple Crochet Two Together (tr2tog)**
   In this pattern, tr2tog is used to form CL, not to decrease a stitch. Yoh twice, pick up lp in designated st, [yo, pull though 2 lps] twice, yoh twice, pick up lp in same st, (yo, pull through 2 lps) twice, yo and pull through all lps on hook.

back

Foundation row: With 5/F hook, ch 120 (132, 144, 156). Starting in seventh ch from hook (counts as dc, ch 2), * 1 dc in next ch, ch 2, sk 2 ch, rep from * 36 (40, 44, 48) times more, 1 dc in last ch, turn—38 (42, 46, 50) ch-2 sps.

Row 1 (RS): Ch 1, 1 sc in first dc, * ch 9, sk 1 dc, work [1 sc, ch 4, tr2tog] *all in next dc*, sk 1 dc, work [tr2tog, ch 4, 1 sc] *all in next dc*, rep from * 8 (9, 10, 11) times to last 2 ch-2 sps, ch 9, sk 1 dc, 1 sc in third ch of tch, turn.

Row 2: Ch 10 (counts as trtr, ch 4), 1 sc in ch-9 lp, * [ch 4, tr2tog, ch 4, 1 Sl st, ch 4, tr2tog] all in next tr2tog, ch 4, 1 sc in next ch-9 lp, rep from * 8 (9, 10, 11) times more, ch 4, 1 trtr in last sc, turn.

Row 3: Ch 1, 1 sc into first trtr, * ch 5, 1 sc in top of next tr2tog, rep from * 18 (19, 20, 21) times more, ending ch 5, 1 sc in sixth ch of tch, turn—20 (21, 22, 23) ch-5 sps.

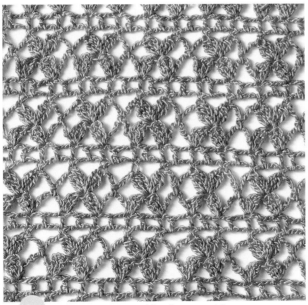

The stitch pattern resembles four-petal flowers growing on a trellis.

Row 4: Ch 5 (counts as 1 dc, ch 2), 1 dc in next ch-5 sp, ch 2, 1 dc in next sc, * ch 2, 1 dc in next ch-5 sp, ch 2, 1 dc in next sc, rep from * 17 (19, 21, 23) times more, turn—38 (42, 46, 50) ch-2 sps.

Rep rows 1–4 until back measures 24" (25", 26", 27") [61 (63.5, 66, 68.6) cm] from beg, ending with row 4. Fasten off.

left front

Foundation row: With 5/F hook, ch 60 (72, 72, 84). Work patt same as back—18 (22, 22, 26) ch-2 sps.

Cont until piece measures 15" (15½", 16", 16½") [38.1 (39.4, 40.6, 41.9) cm] from beg, ending with row 4.

Next row (WS): Sl st in 12 ch-2 sps, making 2 Sl st in each sp, then cont patt beg with row 1 in rem sts. Work on these sts until piece is same length as back to shoulder. Fasten off.

right front

Work same as left front to neck shaping, ending with row 4, turn. Work row 1 of patt to last 12 ch-2 sps, turn, leave rem sts unworked. Cont patt as established until piece measures same length as back to shoulder. Fasten off.

sleeves

Make 2.

With 5/F hook, ch 83 (95, 95, 107). Work patt same as back—26 (30, 30, 34) ch-2 sps.

Cont patt as established until sleeve measures 12" (12½", 13", 13½") [30.5 (31.8, 33, 34.3) cm] from beg. Change to 6/G hook and cont patt as established for 4" (10.2 cm) more, ending with row 4. Fasten off.

finishing

1. Sew shoulder seams.
2. Mark center of sleeve, pin center of sleeve to shoulder seam, pin underarms in place, sew in sleeve, easing in to fit.
3. Sew underarm seams.
4. Work button band and neck border.
5. Make button covers. Sew in place on cardigan front.
6. Weave in ends using a tapestry needle.
7. Do not block.

button band and neck border

With 4/E hook, starting at top right front, work 1 row sc all around neck edge to top left front. Ch 1, turn, work a second row of sc around neck. Fasten off.

Row 1: Join yarn at bottom right corner, work in sc evenly spaced up right front to top, work 3 sc in corner, cont in sc around neck edge to top left front, work 3 sc in last st for corner, cont down left front to end, turn.

Single crochet rows make a stable border for the neck and fronts.

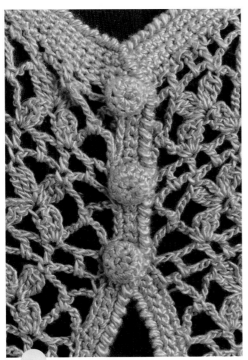

Crochet-covered buttons accent the deep scoop neck.

Row 2: Work 1 sc in each sc to top of left front, 3 sc in center st of corner, sc around neck to top right front, 3 sc in center st of corner, * ch 3, sk 3 sts, 1 sc in next 7 sc, rep from * twice more (3 buttonholes made), cont in sc to bottom right front, turn.

Row 3: Work 1 sc in each st to first buttonhole, * 3 sc in ch-3 sp, 1 sc in next 7 sc, rep from * once, 3 sc in next ch-3 sp, 1 sc in each st, 3 sc in center st of corner, cont 1 sc in each st around to bottom left corner. Do not fasten off. Do not turn.

Row 4: Work 1 row rev sc in each sc, fasten off.

button covers

Make 3.

Foundation row: Using 4/E hook, ch 3, 8 sc in first st, Sl st to first st to join. Do not turn.

Rnd 1: Ch 1, 2 sc in each of next 8 sc, Sl st to first st to join. Do not turn.

Rnd 2: Ch 1, 1 sc in each stc fasten off, leaving 15" (38.1 cm) tail for gathering and sewing.

Thread end onto a tapestry needle, gather up sts of last row, place button on piece just made, pull end tightly, encasing button inside its cover, and knot securely. Use rem yarn to sew buttons in place.

pocket **cardigan**

Classic styling, V-neck, and pockets combined with an easy textured stitch make this cardigan a winner.

yarn
Bulky-weight one-ply

1x & 2x: 1,566 yd (1,422 m)
3x: 1,653 yd (1,501 m)
4x: 1,740 yd (1,580 m)

hooks
10½/K (6.5 mm) for main body
9/I (5.5 mm) for trim

stitches
Single crochet
Double crochet

gauge
5 dc groups = 4" (10.2 cm)
using 10½/K hook

notions
Tapestry needle
Five wooden buttons, 1¼"
(3.2 cm) diameter

finished size
1X (2X, 3X, 4X)
Bust size 48" (52", 56", 60")
[121.9 (132.1, 142.2, 152.4) cm]

notes

1. **To dec this patt,** *on dc rows, first dec will eliminate first dc of group, second dec will eliminate second dc of group.*
2. **To inc this patt,** *add 1 extra dc to group, then add second. When two inc are made, form another dc group.*

back

Foundation row: With 10½/K hook, ch 63 (69, 75, 81). Starting in second ch from hook, 1 sc in each ch to end of row, turn—62 (68, 74, 80) sc.

Row 1: Ch 1, sk first st, 1 sc in next 60 (66, 72, 78) sc, 1 sc in tch, turn.

Row 2: Ch 3 (counts as dc), sk first st, 1 dc in next 60 (66, 72, 78) sts, 1 dc in tch, turn—62 (68, 74, 80) dc.

Row 3: Ch 1, 1 sc in sp bet first 2 dc, * ch 2, sk 2 dc, 1 sc in next space bet dc, rep from * 29 (32, 35, 38) times more, ending last rep with sc in tch, turn—30 (33, 36, 39) ch-2 sps and 1 sc each side.

Row 4: Ch 3 (counts as dc), * 2 dc in next ch-2 sp, rep from * 29 (32, 35, 38) times more, 1 dc in tch, turn—30 (33, 36, 39) dc groups and 1 dc each side.

Rep rows 3 and 4 until piece measures 15½" (16", 16½" 17") [39.4 (40.6, 41.9, 43.2) cm] from beg, ending with row 4.

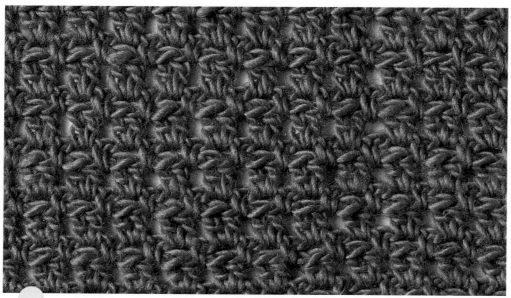

In this easy two-row pattern, single crochet stitches are worked into spaces between double crochet stitches in the row below; then double crochet stitches are worked into spaces between single crochet stitches in the next row.

Armhole shaping: Sl st in first 3 dc groups, ch 3 (counts as 1 sc, ch 2), sk next 2 dc, 1 sc in next sp, * ch 2, sk 2 dc, 1 sc next sp, rep from * 22 (25, 28, 31) times more, turn, leave rem 3 groups of dc unworked—24 (27, 30, 33) ch-2 sps.

Cont in patt as established until armhole measures 10" (10½", 11", 11½") [25.4 26.9, 27.9, 29.2) cm]. Fasten off.

left front

Foundation row: With 10½/K hook, ch 33 (35, 37, 39). Starting in second ch from hook, 1 sc in each ch to end of row, turn—32 (34, 36, 38) sc.

Row 1: Ch 1, sk first st, 1 sc in next 30 (32, 34, 36) sc, 1 sc in tch, turn—32 (34, 36, 38) sc.

Row 2: Ch 3 (counts as dc), sk first st, 1 dc in next 30 (32, 34, 36) sts, 1 dc in tch, turn—32 (34, 36, 38) dc.

Row 3: Ch 1, 1 sc in sp bet first 2 dc, * ch 2, sk 2 dc, 1 sc in next space bet dc, rep from * 14 (15, 16, 17) times more, ending last rep with sc in tch, turn—15 (16, 17, 18) ch-2 sps and 1 sc each side.

Row 4: Ch 3 (counts as dc), * 2 dc in next ch-2 sp, rep from * 14 (15, 16, 17) times more, 1 dc in tch, turn—15 (16, 17, 18) dc groups and 1 dc each side.

Rep rows 3 and 4 until piece measures same length as back to armhole, ending with row 4.

Armhole shaping: Sl st in 3 dc groups, ch 3 (counts as sc, ch 2), sk next group, 1 sc in next sp, * ch 2, sk 2 dc, 1 sc next sp, rep from * 11 (12, 13, 14) times more, turn—12 (13, 14, 15) ch-2 sps.

Cont in patt as established, and at the same time, dec 1 st at neck edge every dc row until 5 (6, 7, 8) dc groups rem. Work even until piece measures same length as back to shoulder. Fasten off.

right front

Same as left front, reversing arm and neck shaping.

sleeves

Make 2.

Foundation row: With 9/I hook, ch 33 (35, 37, 39). Work same as front for first 4 rows—30 (33, 36, 39) ch-2 sps and 1 sc each side.

Change to 10½/K hook and cont in patt until piece measures 6½" (16.5 cm) from beg, ending with row 3.

Patch pockets are crocheted separately and hand-sewn in place.

Inc 1 st each side. Rep inc every other dc row 5 times more—36 (39, 42, 45) ch-2 sps and 1 sc each side.

Work even until sleeve measures 16½" (17", 17½", 18") [41.9 (43.2, 44.5, 45.7) cm] from beg, ending with row 4.

Sleeve cap: Sl st in 3 dc groups, ch 3 (counts as 1 sc, ch 2), sk 2 dc, 1 sc in next sp, * ch 2, sk 2 dc, 1 sc next sp, rep from * to last 3 dc groups, turn, leave rem 3 dc groups unworked—30 (33, 36, 39) ch-2 sps and 1 sc each side.

Cont in patt as established until cap of sleeve measures 5½" (6", 6½", 7") [14 (15.2, 16.5, 17.8) cm].

Next row: Sl st in 7 sts, work patt to last 7 sts, turn, leave rem 7 sts unworked. Rep last row. Fasten off.

pockets
Make 2.

Foundation row: With 10½/K hook, ch 21, work patt as back for 6½" (16.5 cm), ending with row 4.

Next row: Ch 1, work 1 sc in each dc of row 4, turn.

Next row: Ch 1, work 1 sc in each dc of prev row, fasten off.

finishing

1. Sew shoulder seams.
2. Mark center of sleeve cap, pin center of sleeve to shoulder seam, pin underarms in place, sew in sleeve, easing in to fit.
3. Sew underarm seams.
4. Center pockets on each front, about 2½" (6.4 cm) up from bottom, pin, then sew in place.
5. Work border.
6. Sew buttons in place on cardigan front.
7. Weave in ends using a tapestry needle.
8. Do not block.

front and neck border

Row 1: With RS facing and 9/I hook, join yarn at bottom right edge and sc evenly spaced up right front, around neck, and down left front, turn.

Row 2: Work 1 sc in each st, turn.

Row 3: Rep row 2.

Row 4 (buttonhole row): Before beg this row, pm for 5 buttonholes on right front—each buttonhole will take 3 sts. Have first buttonhole at beg of V-neck and last about 1" (2.5 cm) from bottom. Work in sc to first marker, * ch 3, sk 3 sts, work in sc to next marker, rep from * 4 times more (5 buttonholes made), work to end, turn.

Row 5: Work 1 sc in each sc, 3 sc in each ch-3 sp for buttonhole, turn.

Row 6: Work 1 sc in each sc, turn.

Row 7: Rep row 6, fasten off.

A wide border of single crochet rows accents the V-neckline and bold button bands.

bright stripes **cardigan**

Bright stripes of color against a black background make a bold fashion statement. The vertical stripes on the sweater front lengthen the look and draw eyes upward to your face.

yarn
Medium-weight cotton **4**
Color A:
1x & 2x: 1,620 yd (1,500 m)
3x: 1,728 yd (1,600 m)
4x: 1,836 yd (1,700 m)
Color B:
216 yd (200 m)
Color C:
1x & 2x: 108 yd (100 m)
3x & 4x: 216 yd (200 m)

hooks
8/H (5 mm) for main body of garment
6/G (4 mm) for borders

stitches
Single crochet
Double crochet

gauge
6½ clusters = 4" (10.2 cm)
using 8/H hook

notions
Tapestry needle
Five buttons, 5/8" (1.6 cm) diameter
Hand-sewing needle
Thread

finished size
1X (2X, 3X, 4X)
Bust size 48" (50", 54", 58")
[121.9 (127, 137.2, 147.3) cm]

notes

1. **Both fronts and back** of this garment are worked sideways. The back is made in 2 sections, starting in center, working toward outside edge. Each front is started at front edge and worked toward side edge.
2. **Do not try to carry colors across rows**, but fasten off each color as that color stripe is finished.
3. **To inc this pattern**, start inc row with 2 dc in first st, and end with 1 sc and 1 dc in tch, on next inc row, form new CL in added sts.

back

Entire back is made in A.

Left side:
Foundation row: Starting at center back, with A and 8/H hook, ch 86 (88, 90, 92). Starting in third ch from hook (counts as sc), 1 dc in next ch, * sk 1 ch, [1 sc, 1 dc] in next ch, rep from * to last 2 ch, sk 1 ch, 1 sc in last ch, turn—42 (43, 44, 45) CL. Mark end of row for top left back.

Row 1: Ch 1 (counts as sc), 1 dc in first st, * sk 1 dc, [1 sc, 1 dc] in next sc, rep from * to last 2 sts, sk 1 dc, 1 sc in top of tch, turn.

Rep row 1 until piece measures 12" (12½", 13½", 14½") [30.5 (31.8, 34.3, 36.8) cm] from beg. Fasten off.

Rows of clusters, each made from one single crochet and one double crochet stitch, are worked side to side rather than from bottom to top.

Right side:
Same as left side, except mark beg of foundation row for top right back.

left front

Starting at center front, with A and 8/H hook, ch 72 (74, 76, 78). Work foundation row as for back—35 (36, 37, 38) CL. Mark end of foundation row for top left front.

Work patt for 4 rows.

Beg stripe patt:
Working in patt, work 4 rows B, 2 rows C, 2 rows A, 4 rows B, 2 rows C, 2 rows A, 4 rows B, 1 row of C. At end of last row do not fasten off C.

Shape neck:
Ch 14, turn. Working new patt across ch, work patt across row with C, turn—42 (43, 44, 45) CL.

Stripe patt:
Working in patt, work 2 rows A, 4 rows B, 2 rows C.

With A, work in patt until piece measures 12" (12½", 13", 13½") [30.5 (31.8, 33, 34.3) cm] from beg. Fasten off.

right front

Same as left, marking beg of foundation row for top of right front, reverse stripes and neck shaping.

sleeves

Make 2.

Foundation row: With A and 6/G hook, ch 42 (44, 48, 50). Work patt as for back—20 (21, 22, 23) CL. Work in patt for 2" (5.1 cm).

Change to 8/H hook, work 2" (5.1 cm) more, inc 1 st each edge and rep inc every 1½" (3.8 cm) 7 times more—8 inc in all, 24 (25, 26, 27) CL.

Work even until sleeve measure 16½" (17", 17½", 18") [41.9 (43.2, 44.5, 45.7) cm] from beg. Fasten off.

finishing

1. Sew both back pieces together at center back.
2. Sew shoulder seams.
3. Mark body 8" (8½", 9", 9½") [20.3 (21.6, 22.9, 24.1) cm] down from shoulder. Pin in sleeve, placing center of sleeve on shoulder seam, and each end by marker, sew in sleeve.
4. Sew underarm seams, leaving lower 5" (5½", 5½", 6") [12.7 (14, 14, 15.2) cm] unsewn for side vents.
5. Work border and button bands.
6. Sew on buttons.
7. Weave in ends using a tapestry needle.
8. Do not block.

Sleeves are worked from the wrist upward.

Wide square neckline is finished off with a narrow band of single crochet rows.

neck border and button bands

Foundation row: With A and 6/G hook, join yarn at top right corner, work sc evenly spaced along top right front, around neck, and along top left front to corner, turn.

Work a second row of sc. Fasten off.

Button bands:

Row 1: With A and 6/G hook, join yarn at bottom right corner, work sc evenly spaced up right front to neck edge, work 3 sc in corner, cont sc along top right front around neck to left front corner, work 3 sc in corner, sc down left front, turn.

Row 2: Ch 1, 1 sc in each st to top corner, work 3 sc in center st for corner, cont sc around neck to top right corner, work 3 sc in center corner st, * ch 2, sk 2 sts, 1 sc in next 10 (11, 11, 12) sts, rep from * 4 times more (5 buttonholes made), cont sc to bottom right front, turn.

Row 3: Sc in each st, working 2 sc in each ch-2 space, cont up right front to corner, 3 sc in center corner st, cont around neck edge to left top corner, 3 sc in center corner st, cont down left front. Do not fasten off.

Work 1 row sc all around bottom left side, up side vent, down other side, cont along bottom back, along second side vent, and along bottom right front, Sl st to first st. Fasten off.

approx	approximately
beg	begin/beginning
bet	between
BL	back loop(s)
BP	back post
BPdc	back post double crochet
CC	contrasting color
ch	chain(s)
ch-	refers to chain or space previously made, e.g., ch-1 space
ch lp	chain loop
ch-sp	chain space
CL	cluster(s)
cm	centimeter(s)
cont	continue
dc	double crochet
dc2tog	double crochet 2 stitches together
dec	decrease/decreases/decreasing
FL	front loop(s)
foll	follow/follows/following
FP	front post
FPdc	front post double crochet
FPtr	front post triple crochet
g	gram(s)
hdc	half double crochet
inc	increase/increases/increasing
lp(s)	loop(s)
m	meter(s)
MC	main color
mm	millimeter(s)
oz	ounce(s)
p	picot
patt	pattern(s)

pc	popcorn
pm	place marker
prev	previous
rem	remain/remaining
rep	repeat(s)
rev sc	reverse single crochet
rnd(s)	round(s)
RS	right side(s)
sc	single crochet
sc2tog	single crochet 2 stitches together
sk	skip
Sl st	slip stitch
sp(s)	space(s)
st(s)	stitch(es)
tbl	through back loop(s)
tch	turning chain
tfl	through front loop(s)
tog	together
tr	triple crochet
tr2tog	triple crochet 2 stitches together
trtr	triple treble crochet
WS	wrong side(s)
yd	yard(s)
yo	yarn over
yoh	yarn over hook
[]	Work instructions within brackets as many times as directed
*	Repeat instructions following the single asterisk as directed
**	Repeat instructions between asterisks as many times as directed or repeat from a given set of instructions